The Window Light

poems by

Michael Broek

Finishing Line Press
Georgetown, Kentucky

The Window Light

It was barbaric but it was our barbarism
   Ed Hirsch, Gabriel

Karma police
I've given all I can
It's not enough—
   Radiohead, "Karma Police"

Copyright © 2023 by Michael Broek
ISBN 979-8-88838-189-2 First Edition
All rights reserved under International and Pan-American Copyright Conventions. No part of this book may be reproduced in any manner whatsoever without written permission from the publisher, except in the case of brief quotations embodied in critical articles and reviews.

ACKNOWLEDGMENTS

"The Window Light" was published in *Plume*.

Thank you to Taije Silverman for her help shaping this manuscript, for the generous friendships of Michael Waters and Mihaela Moscaliuc, and of course for the love, support, and keen editorial eye of Suzanne Parker.

For all the children and their caregivers who struggle, with love, to make sense of it all.

Publisher: Leah Huete de Maines
Editor: Christen Kincaid
Cover Art: Suzanne Parker
Author Photo: Michael Broek
Cover Design: Elizabeth Maines McCleavy

Order online: www.finishinglinepress.com
also available on amazon.com

Author inquiries and mail orders:
Finishing Line Press
PO Box 1626
Georgetown, Kentucky 40324
USA

Table of Contents

The Window Light 1

The Turtle 2

The Window Light Again 33

The Window Light

Painting around the windowsill
blue, dark brush hairs wet with what
my colorblind eyes might think is saturated sky
but really just discovered somewhere between
cyan and indigo (*the spectrum continuous*
I frame the frame that frames the river
its divisions arbitrary). Yellow sill
blue air where it meets this unforgiving green
flowing east though not really color
but frequency or vibration—my exhalations
a metronome, slow clock waiting
on the hospital ward for release, then stepping
out from this corridor of doors, then another.
Rising, then falling back.

The Turtle

#

The text comes—it reads
police

then
taking then

the road narrows more
than it ever has

pointing my car toward him
speeding elsewhere

my headlights won't reach
from that dark space

under my rented cottage
single bed

this turn
all the way to the dark

space under his
now empty, too

as all the yellow
lines splitting

street swallow light—
spit it up again

#

so, there's the silence
from the passenger

side of a 2005 Subaru
with a rusted hood

and unretracting
seatbelts

the airbag light on
though I don't know

if it's the side
or from the front

that the ache will come
pushing itself inside

and safety
just what it always was

the blinking illusion
and the last word

I'll say something
mumbled

for all these
shattered windows to-

night I couldn't
know was coming

#

there are many doors
on the adolescent psyche ward

keeping these almost people in
(parents beyond reach)

son strips his belt empties
pockets then the nurse walks him

around bland corners
and he's gone

we're sat down in the common
room, every edge

rounded, doorknobs
like sunken loaves

with no arms
for tying shoelaces

or sheets, cabinets zip tied
a wall chart holds names

smudged in dry erase
his name goes up

we sign papers for seven days
already buzzed away

\#

leaving the orphanage
on the world's other side

he had stared straight up at the sky
not in my eyes—

there was a white paper bag
of medicines

in a language we didn't know
and later a white chalk

ball would scream out of him
in the airport

bathroom—a cork holding
back what would come

next after the plane had taxied
to its rest

those eyes, I had said
were soulful eyes

and even then
they didn't look at me

when I was done with my metaphor
I loaded him in the backpack

at 5am because
crying rose with the sun

set out for the woods
and the bakery

fed him bits of cinnamon bun
over my shoulder

like he was a perched bird
screaming down

or else raising
us up

\#

first visit he spits in
our faces

*the kids here are so
fucked up*

he says
the guy next to me

*cuts himself
he punched his mother*

he stares down
at the beige

table & I pour ice water
into paper cups

brimmed with shame
his mother

sure it's my fault
how many times

have I wanted *void*
since I walked away

but there's no time for that
anymore

just getting him home
you fucking cunts

he says
goodbying out the door

#

a rolling boil
had been the marriage

I relinquished
always foaming

like a pot of eggs
in their delicate shells

banging against the sides
and each other

until one cracks & leaks
a stream of white

albumen clouding
everything

in there could be dream
or fog

I reach with the tongs
to pluck them out

the leaking & the whole
place them steaming

in a yellow & blue
bone bowl

walk away to let them cool
the steam of them

heated twenty years
these seeds

these knots of broken
and becoming

\#

pack pillow & clothes
leave my

rented cottage home
return to what

I had left—
the shattered

fake fireplace
kicked in

having been long cleaned
up & put away

the cast iron
pan split at the handle

tossed along
with the shattered glasses

and fists
the running outside to get

away not forgotten
but for a time

shunted aside
because that was before

the call & the cutting
dreams & if he

can come back
at least for now & stay

this forgiveness is
the most dense

green
shoot we'll wave

\#

suicide
proofing the family

home, I cram everything
that could be an edge

or tied like a noose
into the trunk of my car

some things are just
so obvious—

the kitchen knives
the coiled rope

but the hack saw
the extension cord

the screwdriver
and bungees

and soon everything
that could be turned

against oneself—
vodka, bleach

and matches
garbage bags

pencil sharpener
screwdriver

an aspirin
a thumbtack

lighters
anything

glass—these small
death

matters
whatever

lodges in the throat
a word

I don't know how to say

#

it's what the doctors gloss
it'll be a tough couple weeks

first days home Prozac
withdrawal late night

he moans
the light isn't right

seeped under the shades
these arms

are not right
hallucinations

he wakes from and mewls
make it stop & all

I can do is
rub his feet & worry

he'll get used to this
ritual I can't keep up

he rises in the gloom
while we are half awake

cramped by his side
his mom & I lying

in his bedroom among
twisted sleeping bags

grab his wrists
pull him down & he doesn't

know what
made him stand now

rocking in the crib of his legs
it's not me

he says but something
inside me

\#

staring up
from the couch

a seam keeps
blinking open

on the ceiling
where one sheet

of drywall ends
and its mate meets—

I had taped, plastered
and painted a watery thinned

out blue over my sleeping
couch

back when this was
my home—this dried earth

gypsum leaking now
so that a stalactite

formed of coffee grounds
and that gel in babies' diapers

might reach down
a brown translucent

finger I imagine myself
scolded under

careless for not joining
permanent

the edges

#

having pried the glass
from his iPhone

cut by cut
he draws a latticework

across his arm
a climbing tower

of red steps
starting at his wrist

rising each
slash toward

the same bled-out
questions

pain answers
more to the point

what the fuck
are those watercolors

Prozac
Buspar

Wellbutrin
Xanax

& other
pastel pharmas

those swirled
molecular concoctions

staining the green carpet
purple

what are they doing
while outside

the red of Mars
looms closer

than it has in 100 years
water lying

beneath its rock a
swelling of some goddamn art

\#

refusing to return to the school
that screams & bruises

like an orphanage
he begins home

instruction which does not happen
at home but in tepid

public spaces—libraries
with their hushed obsolescence

of too many unwanted
typographies—

an orphan has no past
a widow no future

typeset with colonial I's
and perfect Roman Y's

I don't know any of these
who I am or the role

suffering plays
in what I am teaching

or what I have yet to learn
or surrender

his page a splattered
blankness, caged in white

#

referring to who
used to be your spouse

as *ex* is frowned upon
in the court mandated parenting

spiritless fuck
that was the meeting room

where the judge swung in
and frowned

said *children first—*
my *ex* skipped it altogether

which is not an indictment
but weird

because now we are on
the floor

together keeping our
son's kite string from breaking

though ours has—
his *mom*

I'm supposed to say
not *lover* or *wife* anymore

this naming that is not *life*

\#

life begins to slide
on a 24-hour suicide watch

how do you make dinner
without a knife

or be expected not to drink
nightly

breathing smoke
schlepping to the car trunk

for a cup of wine
his room needs light

so the extension cord goes
back to its electric

holes hoping he's no good
tying knots

in his nightmared
sleep

while I'm on the couch just
fifteen feet

from his bedroom door
we plead with the mobile

crisis unit
that we can do this

otherwise
he's back on the psych ward

and I can sleep here
forever if need be

and for years
from now on

there will be this

#

now in the therapist's office
my son is behind

another door I'm not
allowed through again

his hands in sand
trauma sifting his fingers

play therapy
for the mute

scooping moats
and sand battlements

to ward that deep
hole drowned place

we're both trying to
crawl away from

without knees without elbows
just nails

\#

later, bleeding through
three songs

on the radio
having tried cleaning

knives in the kitchen sink
and failed, I rethink failure

my once beige washcloth
now maroon

I'm back in my bed
not threatened just

beached in my borrowed hilltop
home lest the bleeding

start again its
rude bright heartbeat mess

in finger joint
window raised while the rain

spits its question inside: *What
if this is what I am?*

: a sick pilot

whale swimming
hard as it can for shore

#

cleaning still undone
I don't know how

one man living alone
doesn't just drown

under the wave of his own
desiring—

the dirty spoons
and soft edges of humped

clothes
cresting on his bed

but this is how I've lived
my life—a muddy work site

suddenly frozen one night
empty of people

the buildings
neither going up

nor coming down
erection & collapse

indistinguishable
but if I took a picture

there'd be a swirl of mica
underneath

like sand rearranging
a wet blank sheet

under which my son lies
dreaming unfathomable

dreams
of towering girder fathers

I don't know where he is
hiding

little warthog son
or myself

drifting on the back
of a turtle shell

lightning struck limbs
reaching from

under gray green waters
the arms I see & those

I don't. whose arms
(my arms)

I fall into at night
whose arms he refuses

across this dark & tossed
purpled bed we sleep in

\#

the phone rings
the one no one answers

and it's the mom who's gone to
Jesus saying *your son*

*has been texting my daughter
about cutting*

his own skin & *now she's crying*—
once, there were sun dancers

piercing their chests
circling in ecstasy

before the earth was Starbuck's
an old Nantucket name

when for a year maybe two
going home was just a dream—

I know, I say
I won't tell my son you called

but no one should be caught
in this swirl

of bright lights & bleeding
skin, no matter

they want to share it with the world
and sing. these voices sometimes

must sink

\#

every day I drive
back to watch

him day-sleep, he doesn't
and the brain's folds

keep enfolding
like a comforter

in the dryer
heat blasting

his pee-funk
out the vent

steaming
the back yard

I can't tell
if the fireworks we set

in the driveway last night
were burning off

or lighting up
or if there's a difference

fountains of molten light
scarring midnight

blue pavement black
starbursts encircling smoke

enfolding his sarcasm
and scream

like yesterday's eclipse
I poked a hole through

a postcard to see
he says it hurts

every time I touch
his shirt—sunburn—

as if some lord of light
had scored him with a thunderbolt

which is how
the cuts on his arm

might appear
to a seer transcribing

my defaults
in the divorce decree

but then in the night when
I'm squirreled on my side

he wants his feet rubbed again
large roughed teen

feet knuckles dug deep
toes stroked

and achilles stretched—
the mortal point

\#

he won't eat my handmade
dumplings *go fuck yourself*

and *how would you feel*
if I took away *your* phone

until *you* got back together
with mom

and I still say—eat—
take your meds

later in bed
his head now aglow with screen

and the same song on repeat
he asks for watermelon

saying please & thank you
which is the meds

and maybe space
from his mom who dressed for

the night & left, disgusted with his
fucks & cunts

the repetition of sex the most
ugly he can utter

and if I did what he wanted tomorrow
would he stop

and how would I live then

#

it's his vomit
I clean

off my clothes
his

blood dripped
bed spread I bleach

the spray paint erased
at the body shop

big purple X
he tagged on the car

which could sign treasure
or an unredeemable

past after a super storm
has whisked aside what stood

for home, now
fluids running

down my shirt
the finest fleshy truths

in objects
I could hang in a museum

and label rage
or meat

or a metaphysical water
fall

\#

the holes in the walls
are the size of coffee saucers

salad plates
dinner

buffet truncheons
the whole Thanksgiving table

cloth if it were tacked across the wall
and turkey gizzards

tossed at it
with incredible speed &

determination
the same he uses to squeeze

my finger until it almost breaks
like a wishbone

#

watercolors
by their nature

are dilutions
and his mania

and his rages
are dilutions of a color

I cannot see
but feel—

the blue
and the green

are skin & sweat
I've sloughed

at the gym
and felt in the rain

wetting the carpet
of my car

*so where
are the edges*, I ask

hands on his back
pressing where I imagine

are invisible meridians
lines of longitude on

an old map
inked by older men—fathers

dads an
ocean away

is this what they marked
as important

\#

many men
make a man I suppose

also a riot
a death squad

and an improvisational
theater troupe

a work gang digging tunnels
under the East River

emerge from their rock dens
day over, dusted

and blinking to drag
themselves to drink, wives

their sons
emerge blinking out of

their schools
gums bloody

from the playground of fists
improvising

being whole & hard
not blasted

aching revenge

\#

where's home now
where's that ineffable heart

he walks outside today
for the first time

since coming home
leaving home

I paint his room
crack-house blue she called it

at Lowe's, the woman's
dark eyes

smiling at the joke
he wants a cave, I said

a turtle's dank shell
his blunt nose can poke through

not a shell but his
own hard back

pebble heart
thrumming against this

re-plastered wall
tiny paddles furious

against green water
as I lower

my single rounded
claw inside

to touch his nose—
slumped

down, he burbles to the
top again

\#

today at the Asian market
because I decide

making dumplings
together for my birthday

will mean
something—

he grunts past the cold
cases, rubbing fingers

along the glass
someone else will clean

shakes his head *no*
when I point at

coconut-crème desserts
noodle bowls

the neon green leche balls
but he finds a soda

with a ball at the top
and its accompanying plastic

plunger that shoots it down
inside the glass

and when he tips it back
his throat opening

all I imagine is the ball
the size of a thumbnail

stopping his throat—
for my birthday he

eats three dumplings
ancient sachets

of meat
says he's done

The Window Light Again

I know what drowning
happens when no one is watching.

I count the ceiling tiles. Those
crisscrosses that meet askew.

Inside his room there could be anything
going on—I think if I'm gone one

half hour too long, nothing will be
left inside. What is it really that doesn't end?

Still though, there's frost on the window & I see
someone moving out there, maybe two.

\#

Nothing that hides lasts long.
A rented home. An old oak staircase.

I never want to stop—a river halts, overflows
settles & goes on again.

Still falling, I have no idea what
love wants. The buffleheads will return

soon to my riverbank—that personal
possessive. They aren't mine as

the river isn't mine, nor any galumphs'
treading along the river's shore

in unscuffed boat shoes & entitlement.
He isn't mine. None of them

belong to any other river but their own—
black & white, the ducks slip

under the grey brown muck, their shiny
floating bodies bobbing back again

full of the great green stuff
found waving along the floor.

\#

It's unclear to me whether this living is worth
the expense—then a blue/black starling.

\#

Sentiment won't make the office
coffee perk today.

Buffleheads dying by their downy
drove, anonymously

in the never-ending Arctic sunlight
red spread against

the snow. Tonight, color flattens against
the windowpane

its face—wild with the last bird
leaving town, circling back.

Maybe the last bed we sleep in will star.

Michael Broek is the author of *Refuge/es*, winner of the Kinereth Gensler Award for poetry, from Alice James Books, and two chapbooks, *The Logic of Yoo,* from Beloit Poetry Journal, and *The Amputation Artist*, from ELJ Publications. His poetry and essays have appeared widely in places such as *The American Poetry Review, The Literary Review, Drunken Boat, Literary Imagination, Blackbird, Fourteen Hills, Plume,* as well as in the anthology *Border Lines: Poems of Migration* (Penguin). He has received fellowships to the MacDowell Colony and the Marble House Project, a scholarship to the Bread Loaf Writers Conference, and two grants from the New Jersey State Arts Council in Poetry.

www.ingramcontent.com/pod-product-compliance
Lightning Source LLC
Chambersburg PA
CBHW022125090426
42743CB00008B/1009